Affiliate Marketing

Effective Strategies and Advice for Novice Individuals in
Affiliate Marketing to Generate Income

(An Exhaustive Manual for Acquiring Proficiency in the
Tactics Employed in the Field of Affiliate Marketing)

Bertrand Lavoie

TABLE OF CONTENT

Attain Success As An Affiliate Marketer By Utilizing Affiliate Websites

In order to achieve success as an affiliate marketer, the presence of a website can substantially enhance the recruitment of potential affiliates for the promotion and sale of your product. Assuming that the products being offered are reliable. Please find below a set of guidelines to be followed subsequent to the development of a website with the aim of promoting your product:

Ensure the provision of desired content on your website to cater to your audience's needs. As an affiliate marketer, your target audience holds significant importance, and in order to maintain their loyalty, it is imperative to offer them enduring products. Which you, as an affiliate marketer, have personally evaluated and verified to be effective. "This can be accomplished through alternative means as well:

• Championing High-Quality Content: guarantee that your website provides your audience with groundbreaking information, superior counsel, and valuable resources that will be esteemed and esteemed by your readers. Furthermore, bear in mind that your readers have the ability to click on the provided link, and if the content fails to captivate their interest, they may opt to navigate back and seek alternative information. In order to sufficiently finance this endeavor, it is advisable to adhere to the following instructions:

It is important not only to optimize your website for search engines, but also to optimize it for the benefit of those who visit and consume its content. This contributes to augmenting the volume of visitors directed towards your website.

Conduct meticulous research on your content to ensure their accuracy. The dissemination of inaccurate information on your website can have adverse consequences for your site.

To ensure integrity, refrain from misleading your readership with the content posted on your website. Strive to deliver to your readers the promises you make, as doing so will engender satisfaction in your audience.

Employ visually appealing, organized, and user-friendly designs: As an affiliate marketer who promotes and sells products on a website, it is crucial to ensure that the design utilized is visually appealing and tidy. And not websites or designs that bear resemblance to those from the 1960s. Given that your website serves as a representation of your identity to your visitors or readers. The unappealing designs on your website contribute to a loss of confidence among readers regarding your product.

Generate Opt-In Forms: the creation of opt-in forms facilitates the development of strong connections with your audience and improves profitability by leveraging pre-selling techniques and fostering multiple sales per customer. One significant challenge faced by affiliate marketers practicing email marketing revolves around the effective deployment of the opt-in form and squeeze page, which serve to convert readers into valuable list members. Here are a few essential components that your opt-in form should include:

An Excellent Attraction: This feature facilitates the readers in subscribing and joining as members by utilizing your opt-in form, where they can receive complimentary eBooks that are typically valued at $20. This will serve as a form of incentive to encourage individuals to consider the complimentary offering and enlist themselves as members.

Utilization of an Effective Opt-in Form: devise an opt-in form with an enticing design and strategic placement to capture the attention of your readers without causing any disruption to your content.

Maintain Excellent Customer Service: Ensuring prompt and courteous responses to customer comments, reviews, inquiries through email, blog comments, and complaints is a valuable aspect of the services provided to customers. By executing this in a polite and mindful manner, it facilitates a positive experience for your audience, encouraging them to revisit your website. If you are uncertain about the appropriate response to provide to your reader, refrain from stating "I don't know." Instead, conduct thorough research on the matter and provide an accurate and informed response.

Preview of My Methodology

Upon entering the field of affiliate marketing, I discovered that the widespread practice of indiscriminately spamming links to a wide audience was no longer prevalent (a desirable development, as it was an ineffective method of promoting offers). Therefore, I commenced the process by composing articles and conducting evaluations regarding the merchandise that I was endorsing.

Draft product evaluations remain an efficacious strategy for endorsing affiliate promotions; however, it is essential to diversify the content beyond solely the assessment of merchandise.

Although performing a review should be prioritized early on in order to enhance comprehension of the product, it may not always align with the specific needs or interests of individuals.

If individuals are actively seeking a comprehensive evaluation of the product, it indicates that they are currently in the buying phase of their customer decision-making process. These individuals, commonly referred to as "hot leads," present valuable opportunities for your business. However, it is crucial to recognize that the competition for these leads is substantial, as other entities are also targeting the same high-demand keywords such as 'product review' in an effort to enhance their visibility and ranking. Every individual aspires to attain ownership of that coveted ranking.

Furthermore, alongside composing reviews, you also aspire to apprehend individuals striving to ascertain the nature of their predicaments, and devise suitable resolutions for them. So, you aspire to broaden your scope by transitioning from composing assessments encompassing various subjects, to offering guidance and addressing inquiries that individuals encounter during the initial phases of their purchasing process. We are establishing a path for individuals, irrespective of their current point in their journey, all converging towards our affiliate proposition.

When I initiated my efforts in endorsing affiliate offers, I commenced with Funnelytics and subsequently composed an evaluative account regarding it. As my understanding of SEO and organic strategies grew, I ensured that I responded to several inquiries pertaining to these topics. That's how I started.

I refrained from engaging extensively with social media due to the time required to cultivate a substantial following, and my awareness of the increasing prevalence of pay-to-play models on various platforms. As the duration of a platform's existence increases, the costs associated with reaching the intended audience also escalate. I had limited financial resources during the initial stages. I utilized my remaining funds of $600 to acquire lifetime access to Funnelytics, leaving me in a financially constrained situation that ultimately motivated me to pursue the generation of organic traffic.

As a result of these circumstances, I pursued a career in search engine optimization. Therefore, a significant portion of my efforts in promoting affiliate offers has been focused on organic marketing strategies. Producing exceptional content and anticipating its recognition by Google's ranking algorithm. As previously stated, search engine optimization requires a significant investment of time, therefore it entails a strategic approach with a long-term perspective. Occasionally, it is possible to achieve immediate rankings and experience rapid success, but more often than not, it requires a waiting period of 3, 6 months, and occasionally even up to a year to achieve desirable rankings. Occasionally, it becomes necessary to revisit and augment the existing content.

And while it may be on page 1 eventually, it still doesn't mean it's getting a ton of clicks. Given that only the top 3-5 results attract significant traffic, it is imperative to employ additional strategies.

Currently, I engage in social media promotion through the utilization of MissingLettr, a platform that enables me to strategically schedule social posts for a given article spanning from two weeks to twelve months. This efficient approach not only saves me valuable time but also ensures a continuous and perpetual promotion of my content.

I will provide a more comprehensive explanation in a subsequent section regarding my existing content marketing strategy and the methods employed for content dissemination. Nonetheless, in this particular chapter, I aim to present a concise summary, considering our focus is on marketing and content.

Guidelines for Sustaining Success in the Field of Affiliate Marketing

At present, each partner advertiser is incessantly seeking out the optimal market that yields the highest remuneration. On occasion, they believe a mystical formula is readily obtainable to them. Indeed, it is considerably more intricate than that. Through years of painstaking effort and unwavering dedication, a collection of highly effective promotional practices has been established.

Several effective strategies employed in the realm of web-based marketing have continued to demonstrate their efficacy within the present landscape of internet-affiliated affiliate marketing. With the implementation of these three primary showcasing strategies, you will be equipped to effectively enhance your sales and thrive in the realm of online affiliate advertising.

May I inquire about the three strategies being referred to?

Employing innovative marketing materials to promote each distinct product in your portfolio.

Endeavor to refrain from consolidating all aspects without exception to avail cost-effective web hosting services. It is highly advantageous to possess a website that focuses exclusively on each individual product.

Ensure the perpetual integration of product reviews on the website so that visitors may gain an initial understanding regarding the efficacy of the product for its users. Similarly integrate testimonials from customers who have previously experienced the product. Please ensure that these clients are willing to grant you permission to use their names and photographs on the website dedicated to the specific product you are promoting.

You may also consider creating articles that highlight the key features and benefits of the product, which can be included as an additional webpage on the website. Ensure that the pages are captivating and persuasive, while also integrating prompts to encourage readers to take action based on the information provided. Every heading should captivate the readers, inciting them to delve deeper and even make contact with you. Feature your exceptional focuses. This will facilitate comprehension among readers about the ongoing developments on the page, thereby arousing their desire to delve deeper into the content.

Provide complimentary reports to your audience at no cost.

If feasible, place them at the topmost corner of your page so that they are unmistakable and easily noticeable. Devise a set of autoresponder messages for individuals who provide their personal information through the sign-up form. Based on research findings, it is typical for a deal to be closed on the seventh interaction with a prospect.

There are only two possible outcomes for the webpage itself: either a successful sale is made or the user navigates away and never returns to the page again. By consistently providing valuable information to their email inboxes at predetermined intervals, you will enhance their recollection of the item they initially expressed interest in and ultimately inform them of the closure of the deal. Ensure that the content is directed towards clear incentives for making a purchase of the product. Please ensure that the language used does not give the impression of a sales pitch.

Focus on key aspects such as illustrating how your product can enhance convenience and enhance the overall quality of life. Please ensure that you bear in mind appropriate and persuasive titles for the email. To the best of your ability, please refrain from using the term "free" as it may trigger older spam filters that automatically discard such items without any prior human review. Convince individuals who have actively sought out your complimentary reports that they will be foregoing a significant opportunity by choosing not to avail themselves of your products and services.

Acquire the specific type of traffic that aligns with your product.

Let us consider that in the event the individual visiting your website possesses no inclination whatsoever towards the item you are offering, they will be included among the group who proceed onward without any intention of revisiting. Create written content for dissemination in electronic magazines and digital reports. By employing this method, you can identify distributions that are specifically targeting your desired clientele, and the strategies you have implemented have the potential to efficiently capture their interest.

Make an endeavor to author at minimum two articles per week, each comprising approximately 300-600 words. Through the consistent production and maintenance of these articles, it is feasible to generate an aggregate of 100 distinct individuals visiting your website within a single day.

Be mindful of the fact that only a small fraction of approximately 1% of individuals are likely to make a purchase of your product or engage your services. If it is possible for you to generate 1,000 designated hits for your website within a day, this indicates that you can achieve 10 sales based on the average statistic.

The aforementioned strategies do not appear to represent genuinely challenging endeavors when considering the matter rationally. It entails a modest investment and a proactive effort on your part.

Make an endeavor to incorporate these guidelines within several collaborative marketing initiatives. One can achieve a satisfactory level of income and navigate these surroundings by recognizing that advertisers do not possess unlimited capabilities.

Furthermore, take into account the substantial monetary compensation you will receive.

Chapter 6: Domain Name Registration, Web Hosting, and WordPress

Until this point in time, it is expected that you have given careful consideration to the subject or niche that your blog will focus on. We will now proceed with the analysis of the initial steps in commencing your blog. Initiating a blog is not a straightforward task. Before proceeding, it is imperative to ensure that several factors are properly established. As suggested by the title, the initial factors to be taken into account prior to commencing your blog consist of the Domain name and Hosting.

The term "WordPress" refers to a blogging platform rather than an alternative. The vast majority of successful bloggers are utilizing WordPress in practical terms. Approximately 40% of websites are powered by the WordPress platform. That exemplifies the paramount importance of WordPress. Prior to proceeding with this phase, I would like to apprise you of the requirement for your financial contribution in order to establish and launch your blog.

Do not fret if you are constrained by a financial constraint. It will be exceptionally affordable, and you will quickly recoup the cost. We will facilitate the process for you to initiate your initial blog. We will proceed systematically in providing precise instructions on how to do so.

We recommend making use of all the links and websites listed in this book, as these resources represent the most optimal options for initiating your blog. Execute this segment in a methodical manner to ensure the smooth operation of your website. Keep in mind there are a million different ways to begin your blog site. Regardless, this methodology will prove to be optimal for all individuals.

Stage 1

The primary task at hand is to allocate a dedicated portion of your time. The process of arranging all the necessary elements for your blog can prove to be laborious. We recommend allocating at least one hour before initiating this procedure. Although completing this entire procedure more quickly is possible, it is wiser to prioritize caution and avoid any potential regrets. Similarly, ensure that you have your debit or credit card readily available as it will be necessary.

Stage 2

We have now reached the exciting phase of Hosting and Domain name acquisition. I kindly request that you carefully consider arranging for the provision of accommodation for your space name, as the hosting platform and domain name are inherently intertwined. We recommend bluehost.com as a suitable platform for your facilitation needs. It is one of the most exceptional hosting platforms available. Not only does WordPress provide this hosting platform, but it also offers a complimentary domain. Consequently, there is no need for you to make any additional payment for a domain name.

Furthermore, Bluehost offers a guarantee for a full refund. In the event that you make the decision to host your blog elsewhere, you have the option to do so within a thirty-day period from the time of your registration. Currently, if you are considering the utilization of alternative hosting platforms, it is advisable to thoroughly assess the quality of customer service they provide. Bluehost provides 24/7 live chat support, ensuring that any issues you may encounter with your website are promptly resolved. This sets Bluehost apart from other platforms, where you might have to wait several days for a response.

Stage 3

In the third stage, it is necessary to access the website bluehost.com. At this juncture, I kindly request your attention towards activating the 'commence presently' button. Upon selecting the option, you will be prompted to choose a domain name. Currently, you have the option of either utilizing an existing one that you may have acquired, or selecting a new one.

Once you have selected a domain name, you will then proceed to complete a form with your personal details such as name and address. Please rest assured that everything is completely safeguarded and secure. Henceforth, you shall proceed to a subsequent section wherein you will be presented with three alternative options. If you are new to blogging, then opt for the most cost-effective option available. It will suffice to facilitate your initiation. Subsequently, you will ultimately be requested to provide a username and password. Once you have completed that task, you will be thoroughly prepared in a commanding manner.

Stage 4

In the fourth stage, it is recommended to proceed with the download of WordPress. To initiate the process, merely click on the 'Install WordPress' option, proceed to enter your designated domain name, and then you will be fully prepared to proceed. To clarify, Bluehost serves as the hosting provider for your website. WordPress is the platform where you can modify and publish all of your articles.

Stage 5

We are currently in the process of selecting a subject for your blog. In order for your website to thrive and attract a substantial amount of traffic, a remarkable theme will be imperative. Currently, a majority of unique ones are not available at no cost. Consequently, it may be necessary for you to make a financial contribution towards it.

Merely comprehend that commencing your blog with a complimentary topic is an option; nevertheless, the expeditious acquisition of a remunerative theme is highly advisable. You have the ability to explore subjects pertaining to Bluehost, WordPress, and a wide array of other websites. You can easily incorporate it into your website. Ensure that whichever topic you choose possesses a well-structured composition and can be accessed easily by the readers.

Once you have successfully mastered each of these steps in a systematic manner, you should have a functional blog website up and running. Congratulate yourself, as you have now officially become the proprietor of a blog. As previously indicated, there are a plethora of alternative methods at your disposal to initiate the establishment of your blogging website. Nevertheless, the methods we have just outlined will provide you with the most optimal and cost-effective blog site.

If you are not proficient in web hosting or blog editing, it signifies that you are missing out on a significant amount of potential income and should therefore refrain from jeopardizing its success. The initial impression of your blog's appearance will increasingly captivate your audience. If, by any chance, their initial perception is that your blog resembles an after-school project, then you are unlikely to generate any revenue from it.

It is imperative to possess exceptional facilitation and subject matter in order to generate revenue. You should consider approaching your blog with a business mindset. Ensure that you approach this section in a systematic manner in order to commence your blog on a solid footing. If feasible, commence the application of the procedures outlined in this chapter prior to continuing with the rest of the material. It will instill a sense of readiness for the subsequent portion.

Amazon's Program For Affiliate Marketing

Amazon is the foremost global electronic commerce platform.

Amazon boasts a vast user base exceeding 300 million active members and showcases an extensive assortment of hundreds of millions of products.

The affiliate marketing program offered by Amazon provides an avenue for directing customers who make purchases on their platform to other websites, such as yours.

If your blog posts, videos, social media posts, or other forms of content have facilitated the success of users in discovering desired products on Amazon or making valuable purchases, you have the opportunity to venture into the realm of affiliate marketing.

The field of affiliate marketing has a number of years of existence, and Amazon's participation in this domain through the establishment of its affiliate program in 1998 has sparked a significant transformation in the industry. The affiliate marketer now has the opportunity to earn a commission of up to 15% on each sale they generate.

Affiliate marketing is commonly referred to as internet marketing. It constitutes a mutually beneficial arrangement between an affiliate and a merchant, wherein the affiliate is entitled to a remuneration, in the form of commission, for the sales or leads generated as a direct result of their diligent promotional endeavors. Amazon possesses one of the most extensive affiliate programs. Amazon provides compensation to their affiliates based on either the number of clicks or the number of impressions generated.

The Amazon affiliate program consists of two tiers, namely the associate and professional tiers. In order to meet the requirements for the associate level, a merchant's monthly sales from their website, excluding Amazon, must be below $10,000. Furthermore, they must have a website that receives a minimum of 100 unique visitors per day for a consecutive period of 14 days. Additionally, the merchant must commit to independently sharing at least four promotional posts on social media platforms that endorse Amazon products. A professional individual is expected to meet demanding production criteria, including attaining a minimum of one million unique monthly visitors and ten thousand Facebook followers. They can also capitalize on leveraging additional resources from Amazon.

Amazon does not provide affiliate marketing as a distinct service, however, it does facilitate the generation of income through its Amazon Associates program, which allows individuals to earn rewards by directing customers to the Amazon marketplace.

Users have the opportunity to generate income through a diverse range of avenues, such as inserting hyperlinks to external websites, embedding product links on their own webpage, or earning commissions for facilitating external sales.

It is important to acknowledge that there are certain drawbacks associated with this matter. Several businesses encountered challenges concerning their affiliation with Amazon, particularly in relation to Google AdSense and the terms of service implemented by Amazon. This situation even led to a lawsuit filed by Google against the aforementioned online retailer in 2011.

The Advantages Of Being An Amazon Affiliate

Amazon Marketing entails the strategic promotion of products and services to a targeted customer base, leveraging the expansive reach and capabilities of the Amazon platform. There are three alternative methods to achieve this: employing Amazon product links on an external website, utilizing the Amazon Associates affiliate program, or developing a custom Amazon Marketing strategy.

The advantages offered by Amazon Marketing encompass reduced expenses relative to alternative online marketing channels, the potential for enhanced conversion rates, and an extended product exposure period.
Affiliate marketing entails the generation of commissions through the promotion of products and services offered by other companies on an individual's website or blog. The seller

provides an affiliate with a predetermined percentage or commission for every transaction conducted on their website. This particular online business model has gained significant popularity in contemporary times, primarily owing to the fact that it generally doesn't necessitate any initial investment, coupled with its relatively modest start-up expenses.

Amazon marketing serves as a potent tool for affiliate marketers.

Amazon Marketing provides affiliates with the platform to actively connect with Amazon's customer base and cultivate a persuasive environment, thereby stimulating product purchases. Through the utilization of Amazon Marketing, affiliates have the capacity to devise marketing campaigns that yield referral codes specifically designated for certain products, which can be subsequently employed in their marketing endeavours. These referral codes confer a commission to the user who inputs them whenever another individual utilizes the codes to complete a purchase on the Amazon platform.

CHAPTER THIRTEEN
How can the implementation of affiliate marketing contribute to the economic growth and development of a nation?

Affiliate marketing proves to be a highly effective means of enhancing the economic prosperity of a nation. This strategy has been repeatedly demonstrated to be applicable to individuals across diverse geographical locations.

According to a study conducted by the University of California-Davis, e-commerce companies have the capacity to enhance a nation's GDP growth by four times more than what can be achieved through conventional marketing methods, as evidenced by their sales via affiliates.

This represents merely a fraction of the profound impact that affiliate marketing has had on the economies of numerous countries across the globe.

Affiliate Marketing revolves around generating revenue from online enterprises. The individual directs clientele to a commercial establishment, with remuneration granted for every customer attained and each transaction completed. This encompasses the revenue derived from customers who have been attained through the implementation of affiliate marketing strategies, both in terms of generating revenue from customers who have been acquired and from customers who have been passed on to other parties as a result.

Affiliate marketing is a form of electronic commerce that facilitates the augmentation of product sales for brands by establishing connections between them and affiliate marketers. The associates are typically individuals or enterprises with an interest in acquiring commissions through the online promotion of the brand's products.

This marketing strategy possesses numerous applications across diverse contexts. The enlargement of citizen involvement in this activity has the potential to enhance the economic vitality of a nation. Affiliate marketers have the propensity to generate revenue, subsequently leading to increased expenditures, thereby establishing a beneficial economic cycle for every nation.

While the concept of affiliate marketing might not immediately appear conducive to economic growth, it indeed has the potential to be a catalyst for an economy's advancement. A fitting comparison to illustrate the concept of affiliate marketing is by employing a parallel with the process of purchasing an automobile. When an individual purchases an automobile, they possess the alternative of securing financing through a financial institution or utilizing their personal resources. In the realm of affiliate marketing, it is customary for the proprietor of the content to remunerate the entity responsible for selling their merchandise or services upon the attainment of financial gains.

All enterprises aspire to enhance their revenue and commissions, ultimately expanding and scaling their operations. However, it is often the case that majority of firms lack comprehension regarding the potential of affiliate marketing to bolster profitability. Affiliate Marketing confers considerable advantages to businesses, as it not only introduces a fresh pool of potential customers, but also expands the range of products offered by the company, thereby enhancing future sales prospects.

Chapter Two – Enhancing Your Blog for Optimal Performance
Advantages of Utilizing WordPress

Establishing your blog is imperative. There exist numerous technical guides available on Wordpress.com that can assist you in establishing your blog. However, only a scarce few are truly crafted to aid you in optimizing your blog with a marketing-focused approach. With that being stated, if your blog lacks optimization from a marketing perspective, your likelihood of sustaining readership and converting them into customers will be suboptimal. It is essential for you to take into account the marketability of your blog website. Within this chapter, we shall enhance the optimization of your blog such that readers are not merely captivated by your page during their initial visit, but rather, motivated to become your followers, bookmark your site, and actively seek you out on various other platforms to ensure they remain informed and engaged with the exceptional content you offer.

Your Template

The initial step towards establishing a robust and commercially appealing blog entails ensuring that the appropriate template is employed. Wordpress offers an extensive array of templates, providing a wide selection for users to choose from. In the event that you are unable to locate your preferred options on their official website, you can conduct a comprehensive search on Google to discover numerous alternative independent entities specializing in the creation and provision of WordPress templates. Upon identifying a suitable choice, you can proceed to install and integrate the selected template into your blogging platform.

When making a selection of templates, it is imperative to consider several key factors. Initially, it is imperative to ensure that the template effectively aligns with the aesthetic of your brand. It would be advisable to avoid establishing a minimalist brand with a retro template, or opting for a traditional theme in a modern restaurant. Allocate your focus to the aesthetic appeal, ensuring that it resonates authentically with your distinct personal brand.

Furthermore, it is imperative to take into account the aspect of functionality. The selected template should facilitate the effortless identification of all components by readers. Additionally, it is imperative to incorporate a designated space that facilitates the seamless incorporation of a compelling call to action, encouraging readers to engage with your email capturing service and connect with your social media platforms. In the absence of an intrinsic inclusion, ensure that you can readily visualize an appropriate placement for it within the template, such that it seamlessly integrates rather than appearing haphazardly appended at a later stage.

Lastly, you are required to select a template that is compatible with mobile devices. The majority of your readers will access your content through their mobile devices. There is an increasingly diminishing proportion of individuals accessing your website through desktop computers. Therefore, while it is advisable to ensure compatibility with desktop devices, it is crucial to prioritize the mobile-friendliness of your webpage. Blogs that have not been optimized for mobile devices are swiftly disregarded in favor of those that have been. Please remember to assess the appearance of the template on mobile devices, ensuring that all features remain operational, prominently visible, and easily legible. This will ensure an enjoyable reading experience for your audience.

Integrating Your Brand

As you enhance the optimization of your Wordpress blog, ensure the seamless integration of your brand. In the section titled 'Personalization,' an array of diverse customizations awaits your exploration. The particular customizations accessible will be contingent upon the theme you have selected. Ensure that each of these items has been thoroughly inspected to ensure they adhere to your brand's color scheme, typography, and overall design. This practice will maintain a cohesive appearance of your page and ensure that individuals can readily recognize and associate with your brand. Allocate a sufficient amount of time to diligently ensure that your brand seamlessly integrates in a manner that is visually impressive. Merely applying your chosen colors onto the template is insufficient. Please deliberate on the selection of highlight and base colors and their alignment with your template, ensuring an aesthetically pleasing outcome. In contemporary times, individuals exhibit a heightened sense of selectivity in this regard. Therefore, it is imperative that you pay careful attention to satiating their desire for captivating visuals, as this will significantly enhance their inclination to remain engaged.

The representation of your brand on your Wordpress page is akin to the facade of your physical storefront. If the website appears visually appealing and offers a pleasant user experience, individuals are more inclined to save it as a bookmark and revisit it in the future. In the event that it appears average, they will procure what they require, nonetheless, it is unlikely that they will revisit. Should it appear to be anything less than that, it is likely that they will seek an alternative webpage altogether in order to locate the desired information.

Simplifying the Matter.

Your website ought to possess comprehensibility. Numerous individuals tend to perceive their page as a continuous and evolving endeavor. The intended audience for your website should arrive and promptly understand the desired actions to take and the designated paths to navigate. Ideally, the primary source they should refer to is your blog. Subsequently, upon developing an interest in you, they shall navigate to your about page. There, they should be acquainted with the entirety of your accomplishments. Therefore, if you are operating a store or representing a brand that offers products or services such as courses or handmade items, it is recommended to incorporate this information in your "About Me" page. By doing so, potential customers or visitors will be more inclined to visit your page to explore the offerings you have available.

In order to effectively prompt their response and obtain their email address, it is advisable to keep this call to action uncomplicated as well. Ensure that the provision is strategically placed on prominent sections across all primary web pages, allowing potential visitors to conveniently submit their email addresses and avail themselves of the complimentary offer. This will further enable them to stay informed about your blog and brand developments. Ideally, it would be advisable to incorporate a delayed pop-up feature that enables the new visitor to provide their email address. In this manner, if they happen to neglect performing the action on the webpages they are accessing, they will be reminded to do so prior to their departure. Please ensure that the pop-up allows your visitor to exit it should they decide not to provide their email address. Pop-up windows that lack an exit option are deemed as unsolicited advertising and can subsequently lead to a decreased ranking of your webpage. Moreover, Wordpress prohibits their usage.

The Features of External Integration Offered by Your Company

Ensure that your external integration features have been configured correctly. The final outcome you desire is to prevent individuals from encountering a malfunctioning hyperlink or being redirected to a ClickFunnel or AWeber webpage that does not belong to you, when attempting to enter their email address. Please ensure thorough verification of all creations to ensure their proper functioning. It is desirable that you traverse your blog with the mindset of a visitor, rigorously evaluating each feature accordingly. This will guarantee that you are maintaining optimization of your links and ensuring the proper functioning of all features.

Enhancing the Performance of Your Posts

Ultimately, the posts on your page are the primary driving force behind attracting visitors. People are eager to engage with your content! That is the fundamental purpose of a blog, indeed. Maintaining optimization of your blog posts can guarantee that readers locate precisely what they seek, that each post exudes professionalism and readability, and that you portray yourself in a manner that conveys your attentiveness. Individuals who fail to allocate sufficient effort towards optimizing their posts tend to be perceived as inauthentic or indolent, instilling in your readers a motivation to seek out someone else who ensures meticulous post optimization, thereby maintaining a professional and polished appearance.

In order to accomplish this, it is imperative to meticulously review the text for grammatical and spelling inaccuracies, promptly rectifying any such errors that are identified. It is imperative to also guarantee the optimization of all links contained in your posts, so as to facilitate easy access for your audience to the information, products, or services you are referring to. Maintain concise and well-organized paragraphs to enhance readability for your target readership. Extensive and protracted paragraphs can induce fatigue and create a sense of overwhelm when visually encountered, consequently leading to a lack of engagement from your audience purely based on its appearance. Please verify the dimensions of your pictures to ensure they are appropriately sized and visually accurate on both your desktop browser and your mobile browser. Furthermore, it is essential to ensure their superior quality to mitigate any potential issues like blurriness or color distortion. Finally, select a standout image that is appropriately branded, resized, and aesthetically crafted to ensure each of your posts captivates your audience. It is crucial to keep in mind that successfully capturing their visual attention is of utmost importance.

By considering these factors during the development of your Wordpress website, you can ensure the creation of a robust web page. In essence, the ultimate objective is to thoroughly examine all facets of your page while ensuring its aesthetic excellence for your target audience. The more visually appealing your page appears, the greater your likelihood of captivating your audience, cultivating long-term readership, and gaining followings on other online platforms.

Buying your Domain

Thus far, you should have developed a notion as to the subject or specialization your blog will encompass. We shall now delve into the process of initiating your blog. Initiating a blog entails a significant level of complexity. Before proceeding further, it is imperative that you ensure the establishment of numerous crucial factors. As stated in the title, the initial factors to be deliberated prior to commencing your blog encompass the selection of a Domain name and Hosting. The term "WordPress" is a platform designed primarily for blogging, rather than serving as something else. The use of WordPress is employed by the majority of successful bloggers. Approximately 40% of websites are managed using the WordPress platform. This exemplifies the essentiality of WordPress. Prior to proceeding with this section, it is imperative that you are informed about the manner in which you will make a financial investment to establish your functional blog.

Do not worry if you have budgetary constraints. It will be remarkably affordable, and furthermore, you will quickly recoup the costs. We aim to facilitate your initiation into the world of blogging, enabling you to effortlessly embark on your inaugural blog. We will proceed methodically to outline the exact steps needed to accomplish this.

We recommend making use of all the connections and websites listed in this book, as they are the most reliable resources available to help you commence your blog. Proceed systematically to ensure the absence of any complications with your website. It is important to bear in mind that there is a multitude of options available when it comes to initiating your blog site. Nevertheless, this approach will prove to be the most effective method for individuals of all backgrounds.

Stage 1

The primary task at hand is to allocate a certain amount of time. The process of configuring all the elements for your blog can be arduous. We recommend allocating a minimum of 1 hour prior to initiating this procedure. You might complete this entire procedure more expeditiously; nevertheless, it is wiser to prioritize caution over regret. Similarly, ensure that you have your debit or credit card readily available, as it will be necessary.

Stage 2

We are currently approaching the enjoyable portion, namely, the process of Hosting and Domain name acquisition. I kindly request your thoughtful consideration in providing accommodation for your space's name, as this entails a harmonious integration of the hosting platform and domain name. We recommend bluehost.com as the site that would be most conducive for facilitating your needs. It is one of the most superior hosting platforms available. Not only does WordPress provide this hosting platform, but you also receive a complimentary domain. Consequently, there is no requirement for you to make any additional payments for a domain name.

Furthermore, Bluehost provides a guarantee of cash return. In the event that you opt to select an alternative blogging platform, you may exercise this option within a thirty-day period from the date of your registration. If you are currently contemplating the utilization of alternative hosting platforms, it is advised that you carefully evaluate the level of customer service they provide. Bluehost offers round-the-clock live chat support, ensuring prompt assistance for any website-related issues. This distinguishes Bluehost from many other platforms, where users often experience delays of several days before receiving a response.

Stage 3

In the third stage, it is necessary to access the website bluehost.com. During that juncture, I kindly request you to click on the 'commence' button. Upon selecting, you will be prompted to choose a domain name. Currently, you have the option of utilizing a preexisting one that you may have acquired or selecting a new one.

Once you have selected a domain name, you will subsequently proceed to complete a form with your name, address, and other relevant details. Please endeavor to remain composed, as everything is adequately safeguarded and assured. Subsequently, you will proceed to a subsequent page, where you will be presented with three alternatives. If by any chance you have never initiated a blog before, then opt for the most economical option available within their offerings. It will suffice for you to commence. At that juncture, you will ultimately be prompted to input a username and password. Once you have completed that task, you will be fully prepared with authority

Stage 4

In the fourth stage, it is recommended to proceed with the downloading of WordPress. By selecting the "Install WordPress" option, entering your domain name, you will be ready to proceed. So to clear up, Bluehost is your facilitating for your site. WordPress serves as the platform where you can modify and publish all of your articles.

Stage 5

We will soon proceed with the selection of a topic for your blog. In order to ensure the success and high traffic volume of your website, it is imperative to possess an exceptional theme. Currently, the majority of exceptional ones are not available without charge. Consequently, it is possible that you will have to allocate some funds towards it.

Merely understand that you have the option to initiate your blog with a complimentary topic; nevertheless, it is recommended to expedite the acquisition of a premium theme at the earliest opportunity. One can explore subjects related to Bluehost, WordPress, and various other websites. It can be readily incorporated into your website. Prioritize selecting a subject that possesses a meticulous structure and is easily accessible to readers.

Once you have successfully mastered each of these tasks in a systematic manner, you should have a functional blog webpage established. Commend yourself, for you have officially attained the status of a blog proprietor. As previously mentioned, there are a plethora of alternatives available to initiate your blogging website. However, the methods we have just described will provide you with the most efficient and economically advantageous blog site.

If you lack proficiency in hosting or blog editing, it implies that you are failing to capitalize on significant financial opportunities, thereby rendering it imprudent to risk compromising the success of this endeavor. At first glance, the visitors of your blog will demonstrate a growing interest in its visual appeal. If their initial perception is that your blog resembles a casual undertaking, then you are unlikely to generate any substantial revenue from it.

It is imperative to have exceptional facilitation and content in order to generate revenue. It is imperative that you consider your blog in the capacity of a business. It is recommended to proceed with a methodical approach in order to commence your blog. If feasible, commence implementing the procedures outlined in this section prior to continuing further with your reading. It will instill a sense of readiness for the ensuing segment.

Customizing your Website:

They possess a lightweight and streamlined design, characterized by optimum flexibility and effortless uploading and activation. They augment the visibility of the blog on search engines through their expanded array of features. There exists an extensive assortment of plugins available for websites and blogs of diverse categories, spanning from sports to cuisine, politics to commerce, and digital marketing to products. These plugins can be customized to suit the specific requirements of individuals. Owing to their inherent functional nature, blogs are instrumental in enhancing overall functionalities.

Navigate to the "Dashboard" and locate the "Plugins" section in the sidebar. Proceed by selecting "Add New." The webpage will display a selection of plugins from which you can make your choice. But in the event that you desire any additional plugin, kindly utilize the search function located in the upper-right corner of the page. It will be made available to you at that location. Please proceed to select the 'Install Now' option in order to commence the download process. Once the uploading process is complete, the plugin will be visible within the designated section labeled 'All Installed Plugins'. Please select the option "Activate" and proceed to refresh the page, following which the functionality will be enabled on your website. Additionally, it is possible to obtain the files directly from Google and proceed with their downloading, uploading, and subsequent activation using the exact identical method.

Default Plugins

Certain plugins are inherently integrated into WordPress templates. They are efficaciously operational for the intended purpose. The subsequent plugins hold significant importance and warrant mention:

Akismet

Akismet is the plugin designed to safeguard your blog from spam content. Spamming refers to the act of disseminating repetitive messages to individuals who have not willingly opted to receive such communications. Typically, these unsolicited messages are predominantly comprised of commercial advertisements, unscrupulous product or service vendors, online revenue-generating strategies, questionably legitimate services, promotional schemes, overnight wealth acquisition promotions, and numerous other forms of advertising that are neither desired nor requested by the recipient. They can be conveniently sent in large quantities and entail minimal expenses. Consequently, the recipients are persistently inconvenienced by the promotion of non-existent products and services. Akismet serves as a highly efficient plugin that offers robust protection to your blog against unsolicited comments originating from spammers. It possesses the ability to automatically identify spam comments and prevent their inclusion in the comment section of your posts, subsequently eradicating them within a time span of 15 days.

Hello Dolly

As the inaugural plugin integrated into the WordPress platform, Hello Dolly embodies a sophisticated form of benevolence and optimism evident in the melodic verses rendered by Louis Armstrong. Once activated, it will become visible in the upper right corner of your page.

Additionally, there are several other widely used plugins available for enhancing your blog.

Plugins provide a remarkable means of optimizing the functionality and augmenting the overall discoverability of your blog on renowned search engines such as Google. "These plugins are indispensable for the optimal functioning of your blog.

Google XML Sitemap is a tool used for generating a structured representation of a website's content, which aids search engines in indexing and understanding the website's pages more efficiently.

A Sitemap is an XML document utilized by a website to obtain the URLs associated with it. The webmasters utilize its functionality to incorporate essential information such as the most recent website update, modifications made to the website, and the significance of the URL in relation to other URLs. The XML Sitemap greatly enhances the crawling efficiency of search engines like Google, Yahoo, Bing, and Ask.com. The implementation of Google XML Sitemap enables rapid retrieval of the website upon being searched by visitors. Each new post that you publish will be promptly notified to the search engines through the utilization of this plugin. Furthermore, it provides support for the entirety of the website, including all webpages generated through the WordPress platform.

Google Analytics

Google Analytics is the instrument that offers comprehensive calculations of the website, encompassing fundamental statistics as well as a more comprehensive analysis of the posts accessed by visitors from all corners of the globe. It provides a comprehensive overview of website performance and meticulously records various metrics pertaining to blog activity, such as user-specific post engagement and geographical origin. Individuals with a Google account possess the capability to incorporate Google Analytics onto their blog, effectively enabling them to receive timely updates pertaining to their blog's performance.

Utilizing Product Recommendations
For Enhanced Profitability

In the realm of affiliate marketing, numerous strategies exist to augment your earnings and safeguard the account that you have painstakingly cultivated. The majority of the techniques and tactics can be easily acquired and mastered. There is no necessity to travel elsewhere or progress any further. They can be accessed online at any time of the day or night, throughout the entire week.

Utilizing product recommendations is among the more crucial strategies for enhancing the affiliate marketing bottom line and sales. Numerous marketing professionals are aware that this represents one of the most efficacious methods for promoting a specific product.

Should the customers or visitors bestow sufficient trust upon you, they will indeed place confidence in your recommendations. Exercise caution when employing this methodology. If you begin endorsing every product solely through recommendations, the erosion of your credibility will become evident. This phenomenon becomes particularly evident when suggestions are overtly embellished and lack substantial justification.

Feel free to express any criticisms or concerns you may have regarding a particular product or service. Instead of incurring any deduction, this will enhance the realism of your recommendation and reinforce your credibility. Additionally, should your visitors possess a genuine interest in your offerings, they shall undoubtedly be enthused to gain insight into the positive attributes, drawbacks, and advantages of the product in question.

When providing a recommendation for a specific product, it is important to bear in mind certain considerations that can enhance its effectiveness to your benefit. Present yourself as a knowledgeable and authoritative figure in your respective field. Bear in mind this straightforward equation: The weakening of price resistance is directly proportional to the level of trust. If your visitors perceive and acknowledge you as a specialist in your specific field, they are more predisposed towards completing the purchase. Conversely, should you fail to exhibit any semblance of confidence and self-assurance when advocating for your products, it is likely that prospective customers will perceive this lack of conviction and seek out alternative offerings that appear more credible.

By what means do you cultivate an atmosphere of expertise? By providing novel and exclusive resolutions not readily attainable elsewhere. Please provide evidence that substantiates the effectiveness of the product or concept you are promoting, in accordance with its claimed results. Exhibit prominent testimonials and endorsements from esteemed individuals, specifically those renowned within relevant fields.

Refrain from engaging in hyperbolic language under any circumstances. It is more advantageous to present oneself in a humble and composed manner, rather than resorting to ostentatious behavior and a desperate quest for attention. Furthermore, it would be undesirable to project an unprofessional image that could potentially erode the confidence of your prospective customers and clients, don't you agree? It is advisable to present oneself with an air of composure and confidence simultaneously.

Furthermore, it is important to bear in mind that potential clients are not lacking in intelligence. They are seeking the guidance of specialists and may already possess the same knowledge that you do. If you substantiate your assertions with robust evidence and factual data, they would readily allocate substantial financial resources to support your promotional activities. However, in the event that you do not, they possess the intelligence to thoroughly examine your competitors and the offerings they provide.

When providing a product endorsement, it is equally crucial to distribute complementary promotional items. Individuals are already acquainted with the concept of providing complimentary items as a means to advance their own merchandise. However, only a small minority actively engage in this practice to endorse affiliate products. Make an effort to provide complimentary items that can effectively market your products or services, perhaps even conveying relevant information about them.

Prior to incorporating any recommendations into your product, it is imperative that you engage in thorough testing and evaluation of the product and its supporting elements. Refrain from jeopardizing the reputation of your brand by endorsing substandard products and services. Consider the substantial amount of time invested in establishing credibility and fostering trust with your visitors. A single substantial error on your end could result in the complete destruction of it.

If feasible, kindly provide us with recommendations of products in which you possess unwavering confidence. Prior to commencing, it is advised to assess the adequacy of the product support to ensure that the individuals to whom you recommend it would not be left without assistance in the event of an unexpected issue. Please take a moment to examine and assess your affiliate market as well as evaluate the strategies that you are currently implementing. It appears that you may be overlooking the essential recommendations that your products should possess. The success of your program is not solely determined by your plan of action. Engage in the exploration of product recommendation and join the exclusive ranks of those who have verified its value.

USING EMAIL MARKETING

The use of email as a means of online marketing has consistently demonstrated its effectiveness and longevity. This is due to the fact that a significant number of individuals still perceive emails as the optimal medium for effective communication across multiple channels. Hence, the reason for the transmission of more than 200 billion emails on a daily basis.

In the realm of marketing, it is imperative to possess the capability to generate leads. Leads represent prospective contacts who have the potential to generate sales.

In order for email marketing initiatives to be successful, it is imperative to curate a comprehensive roster of email addresses belonging to prospective clientele. Some possible sources of email contacts are:

General directories

Professional directories

Trade directories

Landing pages

Although there exist entities that offer email lists for sale, it is crucial to acknowledge that their dependability is not always guaranteed. Certain items are procured through unethical methods and may have been employed in the facilitation of spamming endeavors. Utilizing email addresses that have been subjected to spamming campaigns will result in detrimental effects to your reputation, as the recipient of your email may infer that you are also a spammer and consequently proceed to block or categorize your correspondence as spam.

The optimal approach to acquire an email list is through organic means, namely, by means of mutually agreed requests for exchange. This augments your standing and enhances the probability of a favorable response to your email by the individual who has granted your request.

Advantages of leveraging email marketing.

Durability - Unlike other forms of marketing such as telephone calls, email marketing maintains a lasting presence. Hence, both parties can effortlessly make reference to a specific email during their discourse.

Intuitive layout - Emails can be effortlessly tailored to incorporate diverse visual elements such as text, graphics, animations, videos, and more. Through the utilization of email marketing strategies, it is indeed feasible to transmit an email that encompasses your complete landing page and presents itself as such within the recipient's inbox. This results in an improved user experience, facilitating positive reception. In this instance, the user will bypass returning to your website and instead be directed directly to the product's page for a seamless and expedited purchase process.

Efficiently reaching a wide demographic - by utilizing email communication, it becomes possible to craft a single message and effectively reach a diverse range of individuals, such as medical professionals, legal experts, dental practitioners, fitness instructors, and the like. This method effectively enhances your outreach capability while significantly reducing associated costs, such as the expense of sending a single email; meanwhile, it amplifies the probability of successfully converting potential leads into sales.

Methods for implementing email marketing strategies

Please find below the sequential procedures necessary to initiate an email marketing campaign:

Gather email contacts

Create target groups

Segment emails based on target demographics

Establish separate email distribution lists for each individual within your intended audience.

Please proceed with the arrangement of each of these lists within your mail server.

Craft your message in accordance with the intended audience. Every target demographic must be presented with a message that is tailored specifically to their requirements and has the ability to convince them to become clients.

Arrange the timing of your mailing in order to maximize its effectiveness, for instance, by capitalizing on significant holidays, special events, and the like.

Ensure that your content adheres to grammatical standards, is rich in depth and substance, serves as a source of inspiration, effectively persuades the audience, and remains precisely aligned with the intended objective.

Deliver your correspondence to prospective recipients in accordance with the established timetable.

Please ensure timely responses are provided to any feedback received as a result of your email campaign.

Email marketing strategies

The subsequent points delineate several strategies that have the potential to greatly facilitate the achievement of success in your email marketing endeavors:

Tailor your message to suit individual recipients – Incorporating a personal touch is vital for ensuring effective communication. Hence, ensure that your message incorporates a personal connection. Engage in first-person communication.

Ensure that your email is designed to be compatible with mobile devices - According to estimates, approximately 58% of emails are accessed on mobile phones rather than desktop computers.

Divide your subscribers into segments - By segmenting your subscribers, it becomes effortless to personalize your outreach with tailored messages.

Implement email campaign automation whenever feasible, especially as a component of the post-sales service.

Optimize the timing of your email dispatch - Research has revealed that the most opportune period to send emails is between the hours of 8:00 pm and midnight. Additionally, communications dispatched during weekends elicit superior rates of reply in comparison to those transmitted on weekdays. Therefore, it appears that individuals tend to prioritize their emails when they have ample free time at their disposal, enabling them to thoroughly comprehend the content. Additionally, they exhibit lower levels of stress which, in turn, enhances their potential for responding in a more favorable manner.

Maintain a captivating subject line – Ensure that the subject line is abundant in details, while remaining concise in order to be concise.

In order to express appreciation for your committed customers who consistently engage with your communication, it is imperative to bestow rewards upon them. Free gifts can do. This will enhance their number of followers and recommendations.

Please ensure that the email contains a landing page with a prominently displayed call-to-action segment.

⬜ Enhancing website visibility through search engine optimization

The most optimal guest traffic for your associated offers is designated traffic. This infers that the guest possesses a strong interest in your expertise or the specific product or service you are promoting. If your content can achieve high rankings on influential search engines such as Google and YouTube (for videos), you will have the opportunity to attract a substantial amount of organic traffic to your offers.

In order to maximize your chances of achieving high search engine rankings, it is essential to optimize your content. You aim to conduct thorough keyword research to ensure optimal placement of the most appropriate keywords within your title, description, and content. Search engine optimization is an inherently intricate topic, with numerous online educational resources available to delve into its complexities.

▢ Niche Markets

The most effective subsidiary advertisers concentrate their efforts on specific and well-defined niche markets. They construct a website centered on their chosen niche and provide added value to their visitors through gratification. Promotions may be granted for member offers related to the respective specialty, resulting in commission gains.

Selecting the appropriate specialization is of utmost importance. You wish to

ensure that there is sufficient demand for the specialty and that profits are being generated
it. The most renowned fields of expertise wherein monetary profits are consistently generated are:
Wealth creation
Promotion of physical and mental well-being, including initiatives aimed at reducing body weight.
Sell-advancement

These particular areas of expertise are regularly and consistently in high demand. Numerous associate opportunities are available within these three specializations. Nevertheless, these three specialties are also highly competitive, thus it would be prudent to explore alternative lucrative fields. Utilize a blend of catchphrase examination to evaluate requests and approaches to demonstrating that cash is changing hands in the specialty (are their subsidiary offers accessible?).

⬜ Benefactor

A publicist can be best described as an entity or individual responsible for promoting and advocating for their products or services. They serve as providers or vendors of goods and services. These advertisers acknowledge that by recruiting associates, they will gain access to a wider audience for their offerings. A sponsor shall provide remuneration in the form of commissions to subsidiaries for both successful transactions and potential customers that they generate.

 Affiliated Relationship

Occasionally, one may encounter an offshoot rat referred to as a companion identification or a reference rat. When you enroll as an affiliate for a product or service, your distinct affiliate identification is established, setting you apart from all other affiliates. It is imperative to note that certain collaborative networks possess an extensive roster of affiliates, thus emphasizing the importance of this factor.

The seller ought to possess the capacity to establish a connection with you regarding a transaction. Employing an exceptional partner weasel proves to be the optimal approach to accomplish this task. Primarily, when enrolling in a membership program, you will typically be requested to provide a unique username. This is subsequently incorporated into your exceptional companion mustelids.

Your exceptional subordinate mustelid is crucial for the enhancement of your financial incentives. You may prefer to avoid exerting excessive effort in promoting a product or service, only to seek certification from another business partner. Nowadays, partner programs and companies offer a feature that enables you to automatically replicate your unique affiliate identifier. Please ensure that you employ this with precision.

◻ Manager of the subsidiary

Certain subsidiary organizations have appointed auxiliary managers whose primary role is to provide valuable support and guidance in order to facilitate your success. They are able to engage in direct communication with you through the use of email or instant messaging services. It is advisable to maintain regular communication with your subordinate supervisor, as they typically possess comprehensive knowledge of the most lucrative affiliate promotions.

• Remedies • Medications • Therapeutic approaches • Prescribed courses of action • Pharmacological interventions

A treat refers to a small snippet of code employed to differentiate a visitor who has clicked on one of your affiliated links. Cookies are employed for the aforementioned purposes, and the affiliated program or organization will typically include them for a predetermined duration.

Assume that the agreement you are proposing involves a duration of treatment spread across multiple days. This implies that in the event that the visitor returns to the page containing the secure item or service within this timeframe, the initial participant who referred them will be acknowledged for the sale and earn the commission.

⬛ Two Additional Subsidiary Initiatives

A bi-tiered membership program will compensate you with a commission for every transaction you initiate, as well as a portion of the commissions earned by the subsidiaries you have designated. The greater the number of partners you enlist, the higher the likelihood of accruing additional funds.

FINDING THE RIGHT AFFILIATES
When you decide to make your proprietary products accessible for

purchase, it is prudent to establish your own affiliate program at this juncture in order to expand your market reach.

Having your own affiliate program resembles having a multitude of salespeople on your site fabricating your business each and every day. Nevertheless, identifying suitable affiliates requires careful consideration and deliberation.

•Quality not Quantity

The presence of 1000 affiliates will prove futile if they lack efficacy in salesmanship. Should individuals seeking to endorse your product resort to unethical tactics in order to generate sales, this could also have severely detrimental consequences for you. By prioritizing the recruitment of high-caliber affiliates rather than quantity, one can effectively mitigate the potential issues associated with affiliates, specifically fraudulent activities and unsolicited mass communications.

• Their Website

Please review the websites of all applicants. Is there a blog in operation?

Is the content appropriate for your intended audience? Is the website secure? Are they in compliance with all the applicable laws pertaining to spam, privacy, and other relevant matters, both in their country and yours? Based on the information gleaned from the website, do they present themselves as trustworthy and self-assured?

• Their Domain Name

One approach to acquiring information about the individual responsible for the website involves conducting a "Who Is" search. Certain websites may obscure or conceal the desired information. In the eventuality of such an occurrence, it is advisable to conduct further extensive research to ascertain the integrity of the individuals associated with the website, with whom you may potentially engage in person.

• The content and information provided by them • The materials and data displayed by them • The information and content they present • The materials and data disseminated by them • The content and information furnished by them

When perusing the website and reviewing its content and information, does it effectively appeal to your audience in a manner that convinces them to make a purchase from them? What types of keywords do they utilize? Is the content and information presented in a straightforward and transparent manner? Are you confident in the level of security provided by that website for obtaining information, such that you would consider it safe to send your mother there?

• Financial Validation

Another important step to ensure when acquiring an affiliate is to ensure their completion of all necessary legal documentation.

Regardless of your decision to refrain from issuing 1099s due to third-party payment services like PayPal, it remains imperative to obtain this information as it delineates the legitimacy of your clients and serves to validate them, thereby aiding in the protection of your clientele.

Additionally, have they demonstrated their capabilities as proficient affiliate advertisers? When embarking on one's journey as a product vendor, it may be challenging to be overly selective regarding the affiliates chosen. However, it is imperative to ensure that they possess legitimate identities, are devoid of any criminal tendencies, and demonstrate a commitment to serving their clientele with honesty and transparency.

The essence of comprehending this lies in the premise of selecting individuals who are novices in the realm of affiliate marketing. It is imperative to provide them with proper guidance and support, aiming to enhance their ability to generate more sales.

Creating A Website Continued

Previously, I informed you that we will be undertaking an evaluation of a procedure that will greatly assist you in effectively competing with numerous colleagues promoting the same product. We will attend to that matter presently. Kindly provide me with an explanation as to why individuals should choose to procure products from you rather than other individuals who are promoting the same offerings. Undoubtedly, your proposition must possess a remarkable quality, a distinctiveness that sets it apart and leaves a lasting impression. This identifying factor is what we refer to as the unique selling proposition or USP.

The unique selling proposition, simply put, lies in the enigma of the Internet marketing magnates. Through various strategies, these skilled entrepreneurs have devised an exceptional proposal that not only captured the attention of their intended audience, but also motivated them to make purchases from them as successful participants in the online business realm. Therefore, I shall proceed to articulate the following statement...

The level of success you achieve in affiliate marketing will greatly depend on the strength of the unique selling proposition (USP) you are able to formulate. The unique selling proposition stipulates that one should possess the capability to tailor an offering in order to surpass competitors. In the future, you may continue to provide the same product to the same business sector. However, if you can incorporate an element that leads to substantial enhancement, you will likely differentiate yourself from your competitors. Individuals will have greater awareness of your brand and exhibit a preference for patronizing your business instead of choosing alternative options.

In summary, the unique selling proposition is equivalent to adding your perspective to the matter.

For example, consider an associate network that provides a digital publication on wedding speeches. There exist a total of 1,000 affiliates engaging in its promotion, and you are included in this group. The digital book is priced at $50, with a commission rate set at 50%, resulting in a commission payment of $25 for each transaction. Currently, how can one effectively generate a higher click-through rate on their affiliate link relative to others' links? Incorporate an element that enhances the significance of your proposal.

There are innumerable, limitless pathways through which one can accomplish this goal. Your creative capability reaches its utmost extent at the farthest point. Allow your creative faculties to flow freely and witness the extent to which this approach can propel you. One of the most widely used applications of the Unique Selling Proposition (USP) entails the incorporation of incentives into the offer. In the circumstance where you possess additional products to distribute to individuals who make requests through your affiliate link, it is imperative to promptly notify accordingly.

This will contribute to enhancing the value of your proposal. Your offers will stand out when compared to the plain offers of other affiliates. Individuals will make a request of you. People will express their gratitude for arranging an exceptional package. Moreover, individuals will hold sufficient trust in your credibility to seek further engagement with your offerings. There are a multitude of areas of interest where you can integrate the incentives. Allow us to explore a few of them:

Products that have been produced by you personally. Need a few plans? I highly recommend referring to the Information Product Creation Manual for some excellent ideas. You may also make reference to Jimmy D. The remarkable collaboration of Tan and Ryan Deiss, titled Products In The Rough Volumes I and II.

Items that have been developed under your establishment. These are the products that have been custom-produced for you upon your request, and all the entitlements associated with them have been acquired by you upon the successful completion of the transaction. Is it necessary to ensure that your hobbies are taken into consideration when engaging with consultants? Please reference the

Outsourcing Survival Kit, the inaugural electronic publication dedicated to the intricacies of sophisticated assignment contracting for a fee.

The items that you obtained, accompanied by their proficient resale rights or private label rights. Having a comprehensive understanding of the different categories of rights is imperative for conducting online commerce. Equip yourself with the appropriate knowledge by thoroughly examining All Rights Explained, the definitive compendium on this matter.

Joint ventures. Other individuals may currently possess exceptional products that would flawlessly complement your proposal. You have the opportunity to establish a partnership with them. How? Please refer to JV Broker 101 for a comprehensive discussion on the topic at hand.

Need more thoughts? Approve, so how about we say you're in a shopping center, and you're searching for some new garments to wear. A certain store is offering a pair of jeans at a price of $100. An alternative retailer is offering the identical pair at a significantly reduced price of $90. Which store do you intend to select? Would you typically make a purchase from the specific establishment that is offering a significant discount? The aforementioned statement applies equally in the realm of associate advertising. If you are able to provide the products you are offering for pre-sale at a reduced price, you would be capable of attracting a larger number of potential customers. Hold up. I understand your perspective...

Nevertheless, those products do not belong to me. I am not responsible for determining the price. To what extent am I authorized to provide discounts? Certainly, the pricing of the products you will be pre-selling is determined by the affiliate vendors, yet this does not preclude the possibility of offering discounts for them. From where will the rebates be sourced? Considering the prospective bonuses from your standpoint. Let us consider the scenario in which a digital book is consistently priced at $50, while the commission rate remains fixed at fifty percent, resulting in a commission of $25 for each transaction. You have the option to present the identical digital book at a price of $40, thereby deducting the $10 from the commission, which will ultimately be credited to your account. Many different affiliate vendors are aware of this method and are highly interested in establishing a significant partnership with you.

If that is not the case, an alternative option would be to offer a monetary reimbursement to those who submit a request through the provided link. You have the assurance of being eligible for a specified cash back rate upon receipt of your bonus from the affiliate vendor. However, another aspect of this approach involves offering discounts on future purchases. Upon reaching that juncture, you will have received your bonuses, thereby addressing the rebates you are planning to extend. Indeed, this approach will negate the advantages you stand to gain. Nonetheless, given the highly competitive nature of this discipline, its significance cannot be overstated. According to conventional wisdom, progress often necessitates taking a step back before moving two steps ahead. The prizes that will be enhanced will indeed render such a gift truly worthwhile.

What has been delineated earlier constitutes a subset of the currently prevalent and efficacious utilization of USPs in the United States. These are proven and tested strategies that are consistently employed by the foremost affiliates of present times. Simultaneously, you are not restricted solely to them. You have the opportunity to devise and establish a unique selling proposition of your own. You may choose to emphasize the term

"Exceptional" within the Unique Selling Proposition. You have the ability to incorporate your own unique flair into your offerings, rendering them distinct and highly exceptional. At that juncture, you would possess the capability to captivate the interest of all stakeholders within your business, thereby marking the inception of a fruitful affiliate marketing campaign for your enterprise.

Key Strategies For Achieving Success As An Affiliate Marketer

Effectively incorporating affiliate marketing into your website can greatly enhance your monetization strategy and yield significant benefits. It is not reasonable to assume that simply registering with an affiliate network will result in immediate financial success. Although it is possible that this may occur in rare fortuitous circumstances, it is highly unlikely to happen for you. If you adhere to these confidential principles to establish yourself as a prosperous affiliate marketer, only then will you witness the influx of monetary gains.

Have a High-Quality, Information-Packed Website

In order to achieve success as an affiliate marketer, it is imperative to establish and maintain a reputable reputation. In order to establish credibility, it is necessary to

We possess an exceptional website featuring superior content that attracts visitors repeatedly. Individuals have the ability to establish their own blog and commence penning content on any topic of their choosing. It is noteworthy that the online domain is replete with personal blogs that fail to gain significant traction.

The primary factor in ensuring the successful launch of a blog or website is to possess an exemplary design layout that is both coherent and user-friendly. It is imperative that your website captures the reader's attention immediately through compelling imagery and engaging content. If you are unfamiliar with the process of initiating website design, it is advisable to register with a web hosting service, establish your domain, and create an account on WordPress.

After creating your account and successfully connecting your WordPress account to the web host, you can begin browsing the various website themes provided by WordPress. There is a wide selection of numerous theme options available for free, or in case you are unable to find a suitable one, you can explore websites like ThemeForest to search for and acquire a theme, which can then be uploaded to WordPress via your web host.

Devote careful consideration to the theme of your website, as it has the potential to be the determining factor in the success or failure of your site. If visitors arrive on your homepage and promptly depart due to an unappealing theme, you will experience a high bounce rate and fail to generate any traffic.

Absence of traffic prevents one from achieving success as an affiliate marketer, relegating them to a state of aspiring affiliate marketers. It is not solely about the impressive design of your website either. Now that you have captured the reader's attention with your remarkable layout, it is imperative to demonstrate to them the compelling reasons why they should consistently revisit your website due to its high-quality content.

Only when you have exceptional content will users begin to develop trust in your website. As this trust gradually strengthens, they will be more inclined to consider your product recommendations, resulting in a higher likelihood of clicking and converting into a sale. Despite the significant utilization of search engine optimization (SEO) by Google, it should be noted that content holds paramount importance in determining rankings. Initially, acquiring traffic for your website can prove to be a slow and challenging process.

One important suggestion is to ensure that your website is not being obstructed by Google, thereby preventing it from appearing in the search engine results page (SERP). Some web hosting providers, such as Arvixe, offer SEO tools for website optimization on Google. It is important to regularly utilize and update these tools, including submitting your sitemap and checking for any blocks imposed by Google.

In order to achieve a high ranking on Google or utilize Google AdSense, it is necessary to have both a Privacy Policy

Page and a Terms of Service Page. If Google chooses to impose restrictions on your website or withhold ranking, it will pose challenges in generating organic traffic. As a result, you will need to invest more effort in promoting your site through social media platforms. It is crucial to possess high-quality content in order to seamlessly incorporate affiliate marketing links, without appearing excessively forced or intrusive.

The links should appear to be authentic casual recommendations, similar to the manner in which one would inform a friend about a remarkable new product. Should you possess insufficiently compelling content, it follows that users will lack confidence in your website, thereby refraining from clicking on the links, and ultimately impeding the accrual of commissions. After devoting approximately 3 – 4 months to the cultivation of web traffic and a devoted audience on your website, it is opportune to explore various approaches to generating revenue.

Typically, after a period of approximately 3 or 4 months, you will have accumulated a sufficient amount of high-quality content that would enable you to incorporate multiple affiliate links. You have the option to promptly include the affiliate links; however, it is possible that certain advertisers might perceive your low traffic and be hesitant to establish an immediate partnership with you.

Identifying Suitable Advertising Collaborators

Before you jump right into an advertisers program, it's important to outline who you are looking to partner with and how you foresee promoting them on your website.

It is advised to exercise caution and refrain from hastily enrolling in affiliate marketing programs with the expectation of immediate monetary gains. In order to proceed, it is necessary to develop a strategy that outlines the intended direction and the potential benefits that it will yield for both your website and the advertisers.

Inquiries to consider prior to enrollment: What is my specialized area? What categories of products have the possibility to be endorsed on my website, such as clothing, electronics, travel, etc? Alternatively, are there several classifications? It is of utmost significance to discern one's desired objectives.

Once you have completed the registration process with an affiliate marketing network such as JV Zoo, ClickBank, or CJ Affiliate, you will be able to refine the selection of advertisers by filtering them according to categories, keywords, content, and geographical coverage. Each advertiser will have slightly varying program terms and commission rates that you must adhere to.

You will discover that certain advertising partners exhibit more productivity when collaborating with your website and you will derive greater satisfaction from working with them. Discern the associations that are compatible with your needs and possess the potential to manifest as enduring partnerships. The higher the advertiser's level of reliability, the greater your likelihood of achieving long-term success with them.

Only endorse products that are logically sound.

If your website already has a considerable audience and significant web traffic, it is likely that you have a sufficient number of returning users who place trust in your content and actively promote it.

Endeavor to adhere to products that exhibit a seamless integration within the layout of your website. If you introduce a product that appears out of place and completely unrelated to your usual content, your loyal readers may begin to question your judgment and be quickly deterred by the incongruent product placement.

Advertising products that are not compatible with your website is unlikely to generate any clicks, resulting in a decrease in your overall conversion rate. The conversion rate refers to the percentage of visitors to your website who are successfully transformed into customers or leads, both by clicking on the product you have linked and subsequently making a purchase. Products that are not properly positioned will not yield any conversions.

Do not exclusively focus on promoting and selling products without considering other aspects. You are advised to determine the optimal quantity of products that appears harmonious within an article or the entirety of your website. If you are producing an article titled "The Optimal Quantity of Y Products," where Y represents the type of product, it is advised to include only the specified numerical value, X, of the products within the article. Please refrain from including any extraneous items in the article that may cause confusion to the reader, with the intention of obtaining more clicks.

It would be advantageous to your audience by promoting high-quality products that bring value to your readers. What is the reason for individuals visiting your website? They desire to witness and listen to your perspective. They derive pleasure from the content of your website and will subsequently revisit it. They possessed a requirement or an inquiry that required resolution, thus they visited your website to seek assistance. They have expressed their interest in the various products that you have to suggest.

You have the intention to feature only products that are relevant to your website and of value to the readers. Do not attempt to deceive your audience. If you compose a text regarding a subject that ignites your passion, it will be evident to your audience.

It is advisable to adhere to products that you have personally tested and deemed efficacious. Nevertheless, there is no compulsion for you to make a purchase solely for the purpose of conducting a product review. Exercise prudence in respect to the content you are promoting on your website.

Furthermore, you are solely inclined to endorse products that you have verified to be of quality. The most adverse outcome that can transpire is promoting a product in which you lack faith or have not thoroughly researched, only to be confronted by a customer who, following their purchase based on your recommendation, expresses regret and demands a refund, deeming it a regrettable misjudgment. This can adversely impact your reputation as an affiliate marketer.

Ensure the accurate configuration of your affiliate profile.

It is crucial to ensure the accuracy of your profile on the affiliate marketing network in order to complete the affiliate marketing process effectively.

Although it may appear obvious, it is imperative to ensure that your profile does not contain any erroneous information, as failure to do so will result in the withholding of payment from the website. Certain networks, such as Amazon and CJ Affiliate, necessitate the submission of your tax information prior to enabling any accrual of earnings from the platform.

Utilize various affiliate networks

Enrolling in multiple affiliate marketing networks will enhance the revenue potential for your website. It is advisable to maintain diversification at all times. Each niche possesses distinct characteristics and demands specific approaches. Through the utilization of multiple networks, you can continuously evaluate and enhance which affiliate network is most suitable for your website.

Enrolling in multiple affiliate networks will provide you with the opportunity to familiarize yourself with the functionalities of each one and determine your preferred option.

Each option possesses distinct features and benefits, as well as drawbacks.

Therefore, I recommend conducting thorough tests and evaluations to identify your preferred choice. It may require a period of 1 to 2 months to properly ascertain the most suitable affiliate network for your website. Not all networks will be suitable for your specific niche, and you will determine which one is effective as you proceed.

Initiating The Journey On A Positive Note

The product review is the prevailing form of content within the affiliate marketing sphere. You select a product for which you desire to earn a commission, compose a comprehensive evaluation highlighting its advantages and disadvantages, adopting a generally optimistic standpoint, and patiently await the persuasive impact of your discourse, leading individuals to click on your provided link and make a purchase. Now, it is advisable to incorporate supplementary content, apart from sales-related material, in order to provide potential customers with a rationale to visit your website and explore its offerings, even if they do not have an immediate intention to make a purchase. Furthermore, it is imperative to restrict the assortment of products being promoted in order to avoid the impression that you are indiscriminately accepting any and all affiliate marketing opportunities.

In essence, the crux of the matter is that it is imperative to confine your focus to a particular segment of the market, commonly referred to as a niche, as a means to better serve individuals who possess a distinct inclination towards it. Ensuring this aspect is prioritized in your affiliate marketing efforts is fundamental for achieving profitability, as it will help you avoid a haphazard strategy and instead focus on targeting a specific demographic.

Consider available options

When it comes to determining the subject of your focus, the initial topics to contemplate are those that you possess extensive expertise or ardent passion for. Alternatively, if that is not the case, selecting a topic of great interest for further exploration should be your priority. This aspect holds paramount significance as it directly pertains to the significant amount of time you will be devoting to the subject matter. It is imperative to acknowledge that without deriving genuine satisfaction from the said topic, there is a high likelihood that your motivation and vigor for the project will dissipate before you are able to yield profitable outcomes from your endeavors in affiliate marketing.

Your objective is to establish yourself as a knowledgeable professional, if not the foremost authority (as elaborated in a subsequent section), in your chosen field, thereby allowing your blog to naturally attract traffic without the need for continual adjustments of SEO tactics to maintain its relevance. This implies that once you have determined a broad subject, it is necessary for you to deliberate upon the specific subcategories it is associated with.

If you encounter difficulties in generating alternatives, please be aware that the niche market presents plenty of opportunities. Simply input the chosen general topic into your preferred search engine and observe the auto-fill options that arise. After identifying several niche areas that are of interest, the subsequent step is to input them into the search engine and examine the resulting outcomes.

Your objective in this context is to identify instances of competition. If the leading search results consistently originate from only two or three websites, it may be prudent to reassess your chosen niche. The objective of identifying a niche is to enhance your positioning as a trusted authority among individuals who share an interest in the subject matter. This can be achieved through alternative methods that do not involve engaging in direct competition with established experts operating within the same domain. Ideally, it is advisable to examine a minimum of five distinct sources that appear on the initial page of Google search results in order to ascertain that you are not entering a saturated marketplace.

Refine your exploration.

Identify the appropriate target: After compiling a selection of prospective lucrative niches, the subsequent step in refining them to the most optimal choices is to deliberate on the specific clientele you wish to focus on. Identifying your target audience can be achieved through various methods, commencing with an assessment of your own demographic and contemplating whether individuals resembling yourself would exhibit an interest in your product or service.

As with the niche itself, it is crucial to prioritize a reasonably specific segment of the consumer population, as each target group will possess distinct preferences and aversions. For instance, in the event that you adopt a wide-ranging approach to categorization, you might classify individuals under the label of "men." However, it is worth noting that a student who has not yet reached the legal drinking age will inevitably possess priorities that diverge significantly from those of a 40-year-old married man with a family. Should you choose to expand your target audience too broadly, the consequence will be the creation of content that lacks appeal for any specific individual.

Contemplate their challenges: Once you have invested sufficient effort in contemplating a particular demographic, the subsequent aspect to contemplate would be the prevalent issues this demographic is prone to encounter. Addressing everyday challenges is a prevalent motive for individuals to allocate their finances. This aspect renders it an opportune area to explore when contemplating your niche market, along with the assortments of products you intend to promote. Furthermore, it is incumbent upon you to take into account the challenges they face, as well as to carefully deliberate upon the aspirations of your intended demographic and devise strategies to facilitate their achievement of said aspirations.

Once you have generated a prospective array of ideas, it is advisable to revisit your preferred search engine and input the keywords you have identified in order to assess the quality of the search results. It is advisable to input the problems that you have identified in order to determine the individuals or groups already engaged in addressing them. Discovering appropriate problems can prove to be somewhat challenging as the optimal niche should encompass adequate demand, leading to the presence of several existing platforms attempting to address the issue. However, there should not be an excessive abundance of such sites, as this could potentially impede or make it exceedingly arduous for you to establish a foothold in the market independently.

Evaluate the profitability: After identifying several problems that capture the attention of your target audience, you must proceed to assess the willingness of individuals to invest in solving the respective issues. Failing to do so would render any marketing endeavors futile and result in the absence of tangible sales. The most straightforward approach to accomplish this task would involve accessing Adwords.Google.com and exploring the keyword planner tool. This tool enables users to access search results that have been filtered based on different keywords, thereby facilitating the analysis of their frequency of usage. You will not only be able to see how frequently the keyword is searched for but also what the breakdown is like month to month and how easily it is for people to find the information that they are looking for.

Considering these specifics, it is recommended that you proceed to explore multiple existing platforms on the subject matter, thereby catering to the prevailing need for information. While browsing through these websites, it is crucial to focus on those with a thriving advertising presence beyond the use of Google AdSense. Any individual has the opportunity to register for advertising through Google; however, if a website accommodates adverts from established corporations, it is evident that the community is indeed offering profitable opportunities.

Contemplate their thought process: Once you have gained a more comprehensive comprehension of your target audience's demographics and the challenges they encounter, the ensuing step is to deliberate upon the diverse strategies and approaches they employ to effectively address these issues. As an illustration, when encountering individuals within the demographic of individuals aged 40 and above who remain in search of companionship, it becomes imperative to contemplate the essence of this concept from their perspective, as well as the methodology they may employ in resolving their predicament.

Delving into the psychology of your prospective target audience proves valuable in the pursuit of acquiring insights, pivotal in shaping content that genuinely resonates with them. Additionally, this will facilitate your comprehension of the intercommunication within their group, encompassing specific colloquialisms and relevant terminology. Gaining insight into the thought patterns and communication habits of your target audience holds utmost importance in establishing a sense of trust with them.

Evaluate your assessment: By now, you should have a comprehensive understanding of the requirements for servicing the specific market segment and the intended customer base. The only remaining task is to ascertain whether you possess the requisite capabilities to sustain long-term success. First and foremost, it is imperative that you contemplate whether you possess the capacity to continually engage with the individuals you have encountered. It is important to bear in mind that you will have regular interactions with these individuals on a daily basis, assuming everything proceeds as expected. Therefore, if you find yourself dissatisfied with what you observe, it would be advisable to reconsider and reassess the situation thoroughly.

Furthermore, apart from your capacity to handle the chosen niche, it is crucial to ensure a sustained ability to maintain the novelty of the content you will be producing. To achieve success, it is imperative to go beyond generating haphazard content. Instead, you must devise a comprehensive narrative that lends credibility to your actions, particularly to those individuals who possess the utmost ability to expose any attempts at deceit.

Examine the industry in its entirety: Merely because a specific niche currently exhibits a seemingly prosperous audience does not signify that you should hastily engage without conducting further investigation. This can be attributed to the potential scenario where the niche you have selected may have already attained its maximum level of appeal. As a result of this, despite your diligent endeavors, there is a high probability that there will be a gradual decline in the number of customers who will engage with your content over time.

The utilization of Google's trend analysis tool proves to be highly advantageous in this particular scenario, as it furnishes data regarding the frequency of keyword searches within a specified month. Particularly in this case, it would be advisable to focus on segments where the monthly search volume consistently shows growth, rather than those where the highest level of search interest has already reached its peak. Although the current level of search interest for a topic that has already reached its peak may be tolerable, any further investments of your efforts in this direction will yield diminishing results.